#FORTY
be the change

JONATHAN SHAW

Published by Midsea Books Ltd.
Carmelites Street, Sta Venera SVR1724, Malta
Tel: +356 2149 7046   www.midseabooks.com

Copyright © Literary, Jonathan Shaw 2018
Copyright © Editorial, Midsea Books Ltd 2018

No part of this publication may be reproduced, stored in a retrieval system or transmitted in any form by any means, electronic, mechanical, photocopying, recording or otherwise, without the previous written permission of the author and/or rightful owners.

First published in 2018

Produced by Midsea Books Ltd
Printed at Gutenberg Press Ltd, Malta

ISBN: 978-99932-7-687-6

CONTENTS

#1	Exploit Your Current	15
#2	The Management of Perception	21
#3	Choose which Battles are Worth Winning	27
#4	The Power of Engagement	33
#5	Making Yourself Redundant	39
#6	Your Most Complex Machine	45
#7	Reinventing Yourself	49
#8	The Emotion of Negotiations	53
#9	The Solitude of Leadership	59
#10	It's Not What We Say but How We Say It	63
#11	80% of your Fears will never Happen	67
#12	Don't Just Think It, Ink It	71
#13	The Big Fish Small Pond Syndrome	77
#14	See For The First Time	81
#15	Why Grit Matters?	85
#16	You Can Be Your Worst Enemy	89
#17	Food for Thought	93
#18	Technology and Patience	97
#19	Share Your Plans as much as You Can	101
#20	Some Business Tips	105
#21	Learn To Let Go	111
#22	Sabbatical At Forty	115
#23	The Art of Firing People	119
#24	Reward Yourself at Milestones	123
#25	People Who Know Don't Talk. Those Who Don't Know Talk A Lot	127
#26	It is Nice to be Important. But it is Important to be Nice	131
#27	You Don't Choose Your Family	135
#28	Meet the Monkey	139
#29	About Mindfulness	143
#30	More than Words	147

INTRODUCTION

I have always looked at life as a book. Each and every one of us goes through life as though it were a unique one, each wrapped in a different cover. One of the greatest things that we have been given is the knowledge that we are born and the mystery as to how long we will live. What is certain is that each and every one of us will one day die and our book will draw to an end. Our mortality is something none of us can change.

We can however, change the chapters and pages that come before. These are chapters that we write, consciously or subconsciously each and every day.

Some books make a great impact; other less so. Others are not worth writing but are still written. Not every book will hit the bestseller list or be celebrated as ground breaking. What is important is that irrespective of what kind of book we write for our lives, it is a book written by ourselves and not by somebody else. Every book should aim to be true to itself and its own potential.

Imagine for a second that you were born into abject poverty or an abusive household. You are presented with a choice. You can either let those first chapters condition all the others to come, or you could let them inspire you and propel you to ensure the next chapters are more meaningful, more exciting and worth a read. Believe it or not, the best books are those that relate a journey from humble beginnings to impressive outcomes. Books of survival; books that tell of overcoming adversity.

There comes a time in life when you are forced to stop and think. Whether this is motivated by a milestone in your life or you feel you are stuck in a rut, it is always a good idea to stop and reflect. Turning 40, as clichéd as it might sound, was a milestone on a number of different levels for me. This book, was and is the output of my reflection on my personal book. The ultimate journey was the hours spent writing it. Having the opportunity to publish and share it is a bonus. Yet life is dynamic, never static and its constantly evolving through your action or inaction. This is what I wish to achieve through this book. More than a book it is a guide. A notebook to help you look back at the chapters that you have already written in your book of life and look forward and reflect upon the chapters you are about to write. Think of your book as having two parts.

PART ONE is what has already happened. It may involve a lot of pain and hardship as well as a few regrets. You may have wasted a lot of time and fooled about too much and you now struggle to find your real purpose. Alternatively,

INTRODUCTION

you may have had a great start to your book and now want to achieve something more specific.. It's time to start writing part two.

PART TWO is very different to part one in that our mortality plays a significant role. For although healthcare and technology are advancing at an unprecedented rate, we can safely say we will not live for ever. This puts things into perspective. Life is there to be lived. This is a big statement to make yet how do we start breaking it down. The best way to approach this part of our book is to embrace our mortality as well as the first part of our life and use it to better ourselves. It is this sense of the unknown and the unexpected that motivates us through part two. This is the part which we should approach with more purpose and direction.

LIFE IN DECADES – TAKING ON THE NEXT PART OF OUR JOURNEY

Before you begin to use this notebook I suggest you take a look at Part One of your book. One way of looking at things is to imagine that a decade of your life represents a chapter in your book.

Let's have a look at what you have been through so far. In general, your teens-to-twenties mark the decade when you start to make heads-or tails of the world and to develop an understanding of your place within it. It is also the time when you dream the biggest.

Think back at this time at take note of the following:
a)   What was your biggest dream?
b)   What made you happy?
c)   What was your main focus of this decade?
d)   What did you loathe?
e)   What would you do differently?

Take 10 minutes to write your answers. Now!

Next come your 20s. During this decade you were likely to focus on decisions that will directly impact your career such as whether or not you should go to sixth form and then university. Should you live in one country or another or what type of job should you take up. This was your chance to be who you wanted to be at that particular moment. It was a time of self-discovery. A time to experiment, explore and simply enjoy the ride.

Once again think back at this time and take note of the following
a)   What was your biggest dream?
b)   What made you happy?
c)   What was your main focus of this decade?
d)   What did you loathe?
e)   What would you do differently?

This time take a few minutes to look at the differences between your teens and twenties. Try to look at what truly made you happy and see if this changed from one decade to the next. What types of jobs did you enjoy most?

Along came your 30s – a decade of decision-making and consolidation. This is when focus became an imperative and life really started pushing you into one direction or another. This was the time to make an impact, overcome your insecurities, establish your reputation and hone in on the things that define you. This was also the time you started planning a family or decided not to go down that road. It was a time of life/work balance and a redefinition of your friendships.

Once again think back at this time and take note of the following:

    a)   What was your biggest dream?
    b)   What made you happy?
    c)   What was your main focus of this decade?
    d)   What did you loathe?
    e)   What would you do differently?

Your 30s were the greatest preparation for the big 4-0. That's the middle ground (not 50 as one tends to believe). If you consider that most of us will live to be 80 or thereabouts then 40 is really the half-way point. A time to take stock. Re-evaluate and think about where you have gone, where you are now and where you are going.

By 40 you have gained the knowledge and confidence that comes from making it to this milestone which is a tremendous achievement. This may also have led you into the dreaded comfort zone – a place you felt comfortable in your 30s and one you may not have the strength to leave. As a result you will find your 40s and 50s become a replica of your 30s. This is why 40 is such a magical number. It's time to shake things up. It's a decade of renewal and ensuring that we are truly working on things that make us happy.

What exactly does this mean?

It could mean anything. You could choose to see 40 as a chance to wipe the slate clean; to start again. In business, for example, you could cut the umbilical chord and release yourself from a job you don't love and go travelling for six months. You are now old enough to take the risks that you may not have been able to take a few years ago. Incredibly, by doing this you also have to wisdom to realise that there is much to gain by shaking and positively disrupting things slightly.

You could also see this as the chance to take a step back. – to release yourself from the corporate race and focus on

INTRODUCTION

your family or your personal passions. It is this decade that will set you up for what is to come, and possibly alter the course for your 50s, 60s, 70s and beyond.

Whichever way you look at it, 40 is an opportunity. It's a break in your routine that you have been hankering after. It is a chance to consider an alternative which may not reflect the path that you are on today. Will you take a gap year? Make a career change? Prioritise your fitness and health, your family or relationship more? It is indeed an opportunity for positive disruption yet it's not easy as we have been brainwashed to strive towards comfort.

With the power of these experiences close at hand start writing your Part Two today. This notebook will guide you through some simple life lessons that can give you the tools to plan your Part Two. It is important that you write them for yourself and not for someone else. Don't limit yourself to whom you are today, but dare to dream of a version of yourself that would make you proud.

As morbid as it might sound, I at times think of my funeral. If I had the power to overhear people at my funeral, what would they say? What would I want them to say about me? It's really about the legacy that one leaves behind, irrespective of what kind of book we have written during our lives. How many people have we touched?

I started writing the contents of this book as after turning 40 I suddenly felt as though life was passing by me but something was missing. I felt that although through my various experiences life thought me a number of lessons, others I learnt the hard way. Further to this, there are other lessons that I still struggle with and find the need to remind myself about. Reality is that life is not easy and we never know what's round the corner and the more lessons we learn the more we realise how much we still have to learn.

HOW TO USE THIS BOOK

The main scope of this book is not to tell you what to do or how to do things. The aim is to trigger off a thinking process which makes you more aware of what could be a better approach in the long run. Take your time to read this book; you can read the book in the order presented or feel free to read chapters at random. Whilst it's good to read it thoroughly, it's important to allocate time for the relevant exercise following each life tip. This is where you can activate the necessary change.

At the end of the day, it's your book and you are writing it.

INTRODUCTION

Pro-tip – planning is great. It's like having a map when you are travelling. It gives you direction and a reference point, yet the best parts of any journey are those that take us down the beaten track. It is the unexpected that really helps us lose ourselves only to then rediscover ourselves. When we stumble upon something unexpected, or seize an opportunity that presents itself, life becomes interesting and definitely much more fulfilling. Take this journey with me and venture on your Part Two, keeping in mind that it is good and sometimes necessary to veer off track. You will create your map but the journey is more important then the destination. And maybe, the eventual destination will also be different from the one you will embark on.

Life tip #1
EXPLOIT YOUR CURRENT

Just imagine you find yourself in a river battling a strong current. You're struggling to keep afloat and are being swept downstream. You could try and swim against the current but this will only tire you out with a good possibility of drowning. You cannot give up as you will most definitely drown. You are fast running out of options when you realise there is actually a third way which is your best chance to get out alive. You decide to use the current to take you to a safe place. In your mind you quickly map out a route, look for a log and use your hands to avoid the rocks on the way down the river. Catch the current and manage your way downstream until you find a good and safe place to rest.

Being able to use adversity to your advantage I refer to as the art of containment. Contain versus control. Instead of trying to control every situation and spending your life hoping you will never fall into a river, accept the realities that life throws at you and when the toughest ones hit, you are already mentally prepared to contain them and make the best of even the toughest situations.

Applying this to everyday life can be challenging at the best of times but recognising the need to lose control of a situation and go with the flow can help you through some difficult situations and create successful outcomes.

HOW DOES IT AFFECT US?

SCENARIO #1 You can, for example, find yourself in a meeting with a team of largely useless people. I know this happens more often than you care to admit. It is a reality check for you and your gut instinct is to leave the room or just shut-off and detach yourself from the conversations. Alternatively, you decide to contain the situation. You find a way of using the energy around the table to your absolute advantage and after a while realise that by channelling this energy those around the table work for you. Their ideas are better, and it works for you. In time you realise they are not as useless as your first thought. Use the current as an opportunity. Contain it to work for you and don't obsess over the need to control each and every step.

SCENARIO #2 Life is a closed book. You never know what tomorrow has in store for you. From one day to the next your life can suddenly crumble. You could be diagnosed with a terminal illness or someone you love dearly is given months to live. Suddenly, your life is plunged into darkness with no light at the end of the tunnel. You feel helpless and on the verge of losing all hope, when you realise that once again, just like in a current, you have three options. You could give up from the word go and allow the illness to take over and win, spending the rest of your days in miserable resignation as to your fate. Or you could live in total denial, refusing medications, travelling the world and never talking about your illness. The third option is that of containment. You can actually find a way of making your illness work for you. Take time off to reconnect with your family and friends. Help others going through the same difficulties. You could create a plan of containment that will keep you going through the darkest days, ensuring you make the best of the time left. This may not help you live any longer or defeat the illness but it will leave you less tired and drained and relieve the pressure of trying to wish away your burden. This route will afford you better peace of mind reducing the overwhelming feelings and distress.

SCENARIO #3 Your partner may be having a bad year. Things at work are not going too well. For some reason things at home are strained. Fighting has increased and you find yourself in a situation where you are constantly dishing out unsolicited advice. This only fuels them but you simply cannot handle the stress any longer. You realise that your contributions are only leading to more aggression and higher stress levels. This is when you decide to contain the situation. Put yourself into their shoes and try and understand them and how they are feeling. Remove yourself from the situation for a bit and give your partner some space. Be sensitive to his/her reality and find ways in which you could make life better for them. Do not fight, just contain. In return, yoru partner will also start reacting differently and this will be of mutual benefit.

Working on Tip #1

In every situation you face, you think you have a choice between the status quo or a complete and radical change. Fight or flight scenario. The truth is that there exists a more balanced approach which involves accepting that which is unchangeable and manipulating the things that are changeable. Ultimately, it is all about making the best of each and every situation.

The PR world uses the term 'damage control' which is another way of saying containment. The effectiveness of these strategies depends very much on external forces yet also on a life time of building good relationships. So for example if your brand is under attack by the media, you could either take the editors head on and try and control what they write, or alternatively you could use your relationships with the editors to highlight the positive your brand is achieving.

Oftentimes, the only thing you can really control in life is your own reaction. What makes situations good or bad is really how you view them. What makes situations worse or better is really how you handle them.

Exercise Tip #1
Think of the worst thing that could happen to you. Your worst nightmare; the thing you actively try to avoid at all costs. Now, imagine it happens and is totally beyond your control. What will you do to contain it?

Life tip #2
THE MANAGEMENT OF PERCEPTION

Life is rarely about what you see but more importantly how you see it. Your opinions are often the result of your upbringing, the people you meet, your education and your life experiences. Opinions can change over the years, but those that you feel most strongly about, your values, are unlikely to change.

Think about it for a moment. Have you got strong views on politics, the environment, and civil liberties? The chances are you have strongly formed opinions and beliefs that are not easily changed on one or more of these issues.

In many ways, this is fantastic. It is what defines you and makes you tick. As you grow older you realise that more often than not, your beliefs will be challenged by those that have a completely different perspective to you. What you considered for so long to be a 'fact' and obvious is not always obvious to others. Whilst this can be seriously frustrating, it could also open you up to different perspectives thus enriching your life and making it more truthful.

SCENARIO #1 Think of you on your first day of work for a new company; or a dinner with a different group of friends, or a trip to somewhere you have never been before. All three scenarios are bound to make us a little uneasy. If we stop and think we will realise that there are a few things clouding our outlook. Could it be nerves that are creeping upon us on our first day at work? Is there one person in the group who I dislike and who I am sure will ruin my evening? Are you worried as to how the trip will turn out? Is there something limiting your feelings, impacting your perception on your next step? Are you going to sit back and allow your thoughts, your perceptions, dictate how you are going to face a new job, a dinner with friends or a trip?

Keep in mind that your thoughts about each and every situation are just thoughts. It would be a shame to precondition yourself and the outcome of a potentially-positive scenario. In reality you may be proven right but what is the point of approaching a situation with a heavy perceived idea thus choking any chance of a successful outcome. Strive to keep your perception upbeat whenever entering new situations. Keep it positive.

LIFE TIP #2

SCENARIO #2 Perception can dramatically alter the way we approach a conversation or a debate. Life often calls upon us to give our opinion to others, listen to theirs and give advice. We often do this without even realising. It is at these moments that an understanding of perception becomes important.

A friend or family member asks you for advice about a job. It is always easy to analyse and dish out advice without realising that whatever you say will affect the outcome of your friend's decision. In many ways, you do not have to live with it so you can be more liberal with your advice. You do, however, have to be careful as to how you approach the conversation.

To begin with, you must realise that your opinions are just that – opinions and not fact. They may be based on facts or inspired by the truth but once you interpret these facts, they stop being facts alone. When voicing your opinion you need to allow room to manoeuvre. Give yourself the opportunity to look at the situation closely. Put yourself into the other person's shoes and engage with their reasoning and point of view. In situations like this it is best to be a catalyst rather than dictate a course of action. You can only do this when eliminating the barriers of your perceptions.

WORKING ON TIP #2

Your management of perception will come from your ability to see a wider view; to acknowledge it and possibly even learn from it. This will come from surrounding yourself with people who have differing opinions. Richness comes from those who are different to us and keeping the door open to changing your views and perceptions as a result. When you can harness the power of perception and accept that this is not reality but only your reality at present, you open yourself up to new, valuable and often life-changing ways of thinking. It's also important that we do step back and touch base with a self-control check; as passionate or goodwilling we might be there exists the possibility that our opinion is or could be the wrong one.

Exercise Tip #2

The next time your find yourself in a debate, try hard not to throw facts around and instead take time to really see things from the other person's perspective. Put yourself entirely into their shoes and make a genuine effort to understand their reality. Some people would know the solution but they need assistance to achieve clarity or empathy. Empathise with the challenges they face and share their feelings as to how this makes them feel. Once you have done this, find a common emotion to be able to connect upon. Use emotions, not cold facts, they are easier to relate to. Once you have done this, try and invite them to consider a new perspective. A different one. You will see you will leave the debate richer and with a wider perception as well as the satisfaction of having truly helped someone.

Life tip #3
CHOOSE WHICH BATTLES ARE WORTH WINNING

Disagreements happen. Be they at work or in your personal life, your relationships will evolve and often cause conflict. Luckily, as our relationships mature we are more and more able to manage these conflicts as well as recognising one very important fact – the knowledge of which battles are worth fighting for and which ones are worth just simply letting go. Yet, this goes beyond choosing your battles as some are not even worth winning.

Some things are well worth going into battle for. If you feel that a battle is going to significantly improve your life in the long-term such as a significant pay rise or a relationship with the love of your life then it is worth fighting for. This is a fight worth investing in and seeing it through till the end.

Not all battles are a life and death situation. Indeed, most of our daily battles are about things that given the chance we would not even remember them the day after. Or even worse, they are battles that create more damage by the words during an argument then the original cause for battle itself. If you stop and think for a few minutes, you will soon realise that many of these daily 'battles' are not worth the energy of a battle.

SCENARIO #1 – The Fridge Story
'Do you want coffee with that?' she asked in a cold, irritating and emotional voice. I felt like ignoring her or simply saying 'no,' and would have happily added a few curse words, but I knew that that would simply make the situation worse. 'Yes please if you are making some,' I quietly replied. She walked off as though she was carrying a ton of bricks on her shoulders only throwing a 'you arsehole look' on the way out of the room.

It was late, past 1am, neither of us had any intention of going to bed. We had stayed up arguing and the fight had escalated. To be honest, I had forgotten how it all started. One minute we were out having a great dinner and, two hours later, we were locked in battle at home. I was tired and frustrated. The silence of the night was doing my head in. I could even hear the fridge humming away, oblivious to everything. Strange, I thought to myself, how I had never heard the fridge before.

LIFE TIP #3

'Do you want sugar?' she asked coolly. 'Bloody hell,' I thought. 'She knows I stopped taking sugar years ago. 'Yes please,' I said. 'Three.' 'Since when?' she asked.

Now, why had I ruined a perfectly good situation? She had offered me a coffee. Perhaps it was her way of trying to sort things out. 'None, hon, I was just pulling your leg,' I said sheepishly, smiling like a teenage idiot. 'I hope it will be OK,' I thought to myself.

Seconds later she walks into the room with my favourite mug in her hand. I got up to take it, so that she would not have to bring it over but she just kept walking past me. 'Fuck off and make your own coffee,' she said. 'I'm off to bed.'

I sat back down, ignored her and rolled my eyes. She hated it when I did that. And yet I loved her – she was my soul mate and I couldn't function when we fought (and I don't think she could either).

I slipped into bed a couple of minutes later. She was still up clicking away on her phone. I said nothing but curled up in the opposite direction. 'Here, have a sip of mine,' she said, quietly passing her mug. I felt like ignoring her and giving her the silent treatment but this wasn't a game. I had to stop playing games. They only lead to a game over. 'Thanks hon, and goodnight,' I said as I took a sip of her coffee. The battle was over.

WORKING ON TIP #3

It's funny how some of the smallest battles can result in insurmountable mountains to climb when in reality we can avoid most battles in our lives. Concentrate on the battles that will actually make an impact on your life for the better, and not the little points of conflict that will only drain and annoy you. These small battles will not help you achieve more.

The issue is not winning in the short-term. It's about long-term gains. Sometimes it is actually better to lose out in the short term for long-term gains. This is what you should always strive for as this is really what matters in the end.

Exercise tip #3

List 5 battles you have had in the last month. They could be little things, like not seeing eye-to-eye with a customer service representative or your mobile phone provider, or ones that hit home, like an argument with your spouse or colleague.

Think about each one. Did going into battle make the situation better? Did it solve the issue? Have things now improved for the long-term? If the answer to these questions is 'no' then you should consider a different approach. Even if you won the battle, clearly these conflicts did not contribute to your life being better and, ultimately, that is all that really matters.

These are a few questions you could ask yourself before you go into your next battle?

1. Am I going to gain anything from this?
2. If I fight, will this benefit my life's journey?
3. Is this worth winning?

Life tip #4
THE POWER OF ENGAGEMENT

How long has it been since you last sat down to write a hand written note of thanks or condolences? When was the last time you stopped to chat with the cashier at your favourite supermarket? Do you make it a point to say thank you? Probably you do not even remember your last time as today you would simply type 'my deepest condolences' under a Facebook post or press 'check out' on your online, yet faceless supermarket website and speed through the day rushed with no time to engage. Have we lost the human touch in our day to day interactions? Are we in a way also losing out on basic etiquette and manners?

SCENARIO #1 My father passed away a few years ago and as you can imagine this loss was particularly painful. The Facebook and mobile text messages were overwhelming – possibly too many to actually absorb. They were

LIFE TIP #4

immediate and kept me reading for a few hours – difficult hours. Incredibly, these messages do make a difference. A few days after his passing, a few cards came through the post. The cards and the words were beautifully crafted and the sentiments real. The thought of the effort to write and send a card, as simple as it can be was incredibly touching. It suddenly dawned on me. Has social media and the smart phone made us insensitive to the small things that matter? Have we lost touch with these small gestures that make all the difference?

SCENARIO #2 People who know me know that I am happy to assist with connecting people and help make things happen. Be it a contact or a lead, I do it genuinely out of friendship but also to add value to friendship and acquaintances. I do this out of goodwill and when it also transpires in a business transaction I do not expect any financial remuneration. Yet, I must admit that receiving some sort of feedback or a thank you call or message is appreciated. Nonetheless, most times people don't bother. I work hard so it does not upset me and yet I still assist and do the right thing when people help me. Besides engagement it boils down to manners.

WORKING ON TIP #4

In digital marketing, we increasingly talk about impressions. We can check everything. How many people and who has seen an advert, how many have actually clicked on a link and if they actually followed through with a purchase. In regular print media this is equivalent to a print run or copies and in TV viewership. These are purely numbers but what matters is quality. It is the power of engagement that will elevate a marketing campaign to generate results and convert impressions into actual leads.

The concept of engaging with people can easily be applied to our daily lives. Studies have shown that it is these meaningful relationships that add value to our lives, beyond financial and business success. If you do not have anyone to share this success with then life can be quite vacant.

In reality, relationships are very hard work. Time and patience is key. In a world where everything is here and now at the touch of a button, relationship building is not something that comes easily to many people, yet it is really the secret to any meaningful life.

Try and look at why you are not able to create meaningful relationships. Are you waiting for people to engage with you rather than taking stock and engaging with them for a change? Try calling up an old friend and asking them to meet up. Offer them help if you know they are going through a rough patch. Make an effort not to speak about yourself and ask questions about the other person and engage with them on a different level.

As more of our lives are spent online, real human engagement is fast becoming a luxury or dare I say, a rarity. Use this to your advantage. Engage with people directly. Whether you are doing it for a brand, a friendship, a relationship at work, go that extra mile and engage. Do not just push your message without thinking of how to craft it. It will set you apart from the rest. We are living in the most connected world ever but also the most disconnected. Make a connection, write a letter or a short note and you'll see what a difference it will make.

> ### *Exercise Tip #4*
> List down a name for each category and think of an action that will really engage them (and follow through... why not?)
>
> - A Family member;
> - A Colleague;
> - A Neighbour;
> - A Friend;
> - A Customer;
> - An old Friend.

Life tip #5
MAKING YOURSELF REDUNDANT

Learning to make yourself redundant is a big lesson you can learn in life, and like all best lessons it is the secret to success. When most people are given an important job or some managerial responsibility, your immediate temptation is to make yourself indispensable. You want to make sure your boss cannot fire you. You want them to tell you how crucial you are to the wider task at hand. You want to feel like they cannot do it without you. Now here's the catch. You may think for a while that this is the way to self-preservation on the job. A way to ensure you are never fired or threatened. It is, however also the easiest way to stagnation and ultimately unhappiness. On the one hand you may think that you are cleverly paving the way for your next promotion, when in fact you are actually setting yourself up to failure and becoming a victim of your success. If you do a job too well and you're the only one who can do it, why would your boss risk giving you a different job or a different challenge? This concept is also extremely valid for a family business. If you are the senior member it's important to plan for succession and the best way is not only to plan your redundancy but make it happen earlier then expected.

The key to real success is to make yourself redundant. Redundant not in the sense that you are no longer needed and can be discarded, or you make yourself a liability. Redundant in the sense that you can safely move onto the next big project or simply onto other things with the confidence that all you have set up will not be undone.

SCENARIO #1 Think of a team you are heading. You have chosen the members of the team well enough to know that you will not be threatened. Yet after a few years you are feeling trapped as you find that you cannot plan ahead and work on new projects as the team depends on you for direction for everything. You regret not having trained them to do your job as well as you do.

You look back and realise that the success of your team is your success and realise that you can grow and develop only by ensuring that your team is as good if not better than you. This is what makes a great leader. The ability to ensure that each year you can focus your energy on training and empowering your team through a careful balance of delegation and oversight is fundamental to a successful team. Letting go is hard especially when the responsibility is great. However, it is only by letting go and allowing your team to make the same mistakes you were able to make when getting to your position, that you can move forward.

Picture a family business where the original founder struggles to entrust the day to day operations into the hands of his/her children. By staying on, the founder not only delays retirement but also jeopardises the business by not letting it experience a new direction. We've all seen businesses fail because the older generation refuse to let go or because the younger generation feel stifled. In this scenario they either move out of the family business or when its their time to run it they lack the necessary experience or support.

SCENARIO #2 Visualise a mother who has kept her children very close to her growing up, perhaps to the point of being overbearing and over controlling. If her children are not given the chance to make mistakes, it is not difficult to imagine why they might grow up to feel unprepared for life or resentful toward their parents.

The sooner you are able to do this as a parent, the sooner your children are able to gain independence and the sooner you are able to rediscover a new role for yourself.

Parents who try to parent their whole lives will probably force their children out of their lives instead.

The same applies for other relationships, including romantic ones. Instead of making your partner reliant on you, empower them to be their own person and to find fulfilment without you. This will probably keep them closer than ever. As the saying goes – if you really love someone, set them free. Great things will result.

WORKING ON TIP #5

If the thought of letting go really scares you, you may have to reconcile the fact that mistakes are a fundamental part of life. They are also the part of life which accompanies the most learning. If you are afraid to really leave things in the hands of your best employee, team member or child, you are not giving them the opportunity to prove themselves or to learn from the mistakes that they could make.

But why is making yourself redundant so important? Can't you just stay in control and do the best with the task at hand?

No matter how good you are, every business, project or job needs fresh blood and new ideas. If you've occupied a role for years, the chances are that you are no longer giving it the energy it needs. It also means that you are no longer on the path to reaching personal fulfilment because you are not moving forward. Worst of all, if you don't make yourself redundant, someone else might. If you are not able to move forward, it will happen anyway but not as a stepping stone to something bigger and better.

Exercise Tip #5

Write a job description of your work. Think of what you do each day, be it at home or at work. Then look back at this list and see how long you have been doing this work for and see if you can visualise a situation where someone in your team or family can do it for you, maybe not as good as you but they have the potential to get there. Work on trying to train someone to do the job and then try your hand at letting go. Then draw up a list of things that you wish you have time to do and see which list excites you the most. The old list of things you have been doing for ages, or the new list full of promise and excitement?

Life tip #6
YOUR MOST COMPLEX MACHINE

The old saying says 'prevention is better than cure', yet how many times do we let our lives pass us by without taking the necessary precautions to ensure we anticipate issues – be they health issues or problems at home, structural or otherwise?

SCENARIO #1 You are in traffic, driving your car when a red light bleeps and warns you that something is not quite right or it is time to take your car for a service. Some will schedule the service immediately and others will take a couple of days to get it done. Nonetheless, they get it done. Few will ignore the warning signals and never get down to doing it resulting in escalating engine problems which are much worse than had they taken action immediately.

SCENARIO #2 Believe it or not most of us will react to a flashing service light on our car or a problem with our mobile. Can you imagine living without a car or a mobile in this day and age? We take action immediately to ensure we don't have to visit this scenario. Our body, on the other hand is a different story. How many of us have had incessant headaches, or passed blood with our urine or worse still have a niggling back pain we have ignored in the hope that it will eventually pass. For some reason most of us simply overlook our body in the hope that it will always work for us, yet when it doesn't it is sometimes too late to take action. Regular check-ups don't always give us all the answers, yet after a certain age they can more than prevent the escalation of health issues and make addressing them much easier.

WORKING ON TIP #6

The same can be said of our mental well-being. Have we been concentrating too much on work to the detriment of what makes us truly happy? When was the last time we took a long break just for the sake of a break? When is the last time we actually stopped to think? Do you make it a point to sit back and be aware of your breathing? Often times we are working on overdrive, without stopping to assess where we are at. We look after our houses and cars to ensure they work for us but rarely stop to keep our most complex machine – our body – is working for us and will continue to do so?

> **Exercise Tip #6**
>
> Take a few minutes to answer the following questions
>
> 1. Have you serviced your car in the past 12 months? Y/N
> 2. Have you been to a medical check-up in the past 12 months? Y/N
> 3. Do you have your next medical check-up scheduled and booked? Y/N

Life tip #7
REINVENTING YOURSELF

Change is easy when it is forced upon us. Isn't it funny how quickly you can lose weight and start going out more after a breakup? Or how easily you would change your life if you were told you old had six more months to live? A workaholic could suddenly find time to travel and enjoy their family. An introvert could change overnight and make sure they spend the rest of their days living on their own terms. An obese smoker could suddenly become a smoke-free fitness freak after a severe health scare.

SCENARIO #1 Imagine a scenario where you have been in the same job for the last ten years. Same job, same people, same position. Ever since you left university you have only ever been exposed to the same company. On the one hand you have always felt safe and secure in the knowledge that you are in it for the long haul and you can safely enjoy your comfort zone. On the other hand, there is something missing. Each and every morning you wake up hoping the day would be slightly different to yesterday, yet it never disappoints. Consistency and safety is what you sought and so you have it. Imagine the company is suddenly sold and you are made redundant. You will most definitely be struck by panic and understandably so. Yet after a while you realise that this is probably the best thing that could have happened. You have been shaken from your slumber and forced to realise that there are other jobs, other companies and yes, that you can actually be more fulfilled and happier. Now is the time to start working on your terms.

SCENARIO #2 Think of any man or woman on his or her deathbed. This is really a time to look back at one's life and cherish those moments that truly made a difference. How many do you think will involve work? How relevant is work at this stage? The chances are many will look back at those memories that were full of meaning, love and comfort. Memories with our loved ones and our family and close friends. For those that worked too hard and made work the focus of their lives, nearing the end will never bring back those missed opportunities, those missed moments which could make an impact on our lives and truly change them for the better.

WORKING ON TIP #7

In reality, many of our reinventions happen a little too late. But why wait? Isn't it better to reinvent yourself on your own terms?

Sometimes we don't reinvent ourselves because we wish to wait for the approval of others. After spending years in medical school to become a doctor, it is hard to explain why you wish to give it up and become an artist instead. What would people think? But maybe, just maybe, this is exactly what you should be doing and you shouldn't be waiting for anybody's approval as often this approval is conditioned by the fact that many will not have the courage to take the step you are taking.

Other people rarely have a full picture of our potential. We know ourselves the best so if we feel the time is right for reinvention it probably is. After all, you could be dead in six months time without warning from your doctor. Why wait?

Exercise Tip #7

Write down a list of 10 things you would change about your life if you only had six months left to live. After your list is done make sure you do at least two of them before the end of the year.

Life tip #8
THE EMOTION OF NEGOTIATIONS

We constantly negotiate. We negotiate with others, for others and with external forces such as time. We also negotiate with ourselves. Negotiation is really an art, one that we rarely get trained to do unless through experience and oftentimes multiple errors. More often than not we are not given a second chance to negotiate something. You negotiate badly – you lose.

Learning to negotiate, often through your own mistakes and losses is a roller coaster ride of emotions. From the smallest negotiation on a micro level to the negotiation of a business deal which could earn you or cost you millions, negotiation in its essence remains the same. Underpinning each move is a great deal of emotion that can make or break you. Being aware of this emotional exposure is an important start to understanding the art of a good negotiation.

LIFE TIP #8

Once you have harnessed your emotions then you can focus on the most crucial element of the negotiation which is building a rapport. This, whilst keeping in mind the fact that the other party is also going through the same emotional journey even if it is distinct to your own. A rapport is fundamental in any negotiation as it is the only thing that allows for that extra leeway that brings you to a compromise. Should this space not be present then negotiation becomes harder and oftentimes fails.

As soon as you have managed the emotion of negotiation, it is then technique that will determine the outcome. Many books have been written on the subject yet when push comes to shove I always go by three main rules:

a) Avoid putting all your cards on the table first be it a selling price, an offer or a salary package
b) Have red lines but prepare to be flexible keeping the bigger picture in mind;
c) Once it's done; its done. Yes, learn and evaluate what you could have done better but do not get stuck in a negative rut if you think you could have done a better deal. Move on.

SCENARIO #1 Think of a negotiation between a couple going through a separation agreement. Emotions are running high and oftentimes overshadow each aspect of the agreement. Many will tell you that had they known how to manage their emotions and concentrate on the bigger picture and the actual negotiation itself their agreement would have been much faster and definitely less painful. This is naturally one extreme as understandably so it is hard after much history to sit across a table and negotiate for something that was yours in the first place. An understanding of our emotions however can take us a long way.

SCENARIO #2 Think back at your first house and the negotiations you went through to buy it. It was a fantastic deal and you were battling with another two couples to purchase it. You are convinced it is the right house for you but your budget is slightly below the asking price. The couple selling the house are young and affable and you decide to get to know them a little, and develop a rapport before discussion price. They take a liking to you and your plans for the house and cannot imagine anyone else living there. The house is sold. Before the price is discussed the sellers have made their decision on an emotional connection first. Building relationships pay in the long-run pays.

WORKING ON TIP #8

Building relationships is the cornerstone of most of the successes that we will register through our lives. As we can see this also extends to successful negotiations. It is not always easy especially when negotiating for personal things, for example the purchase of a house or a separation or a divorce. We can easily fall into the trap of being too eager and impatient as well as allowing for our emotions to get the better of us. Yet, whichever part you are on, preparation is key. Prepare yourself by outlining the limits that you will accept and most importantly, prepare yourself to build a rapport with the other party. If you are the buyer, for example, try and avoid two main pitfalls. Avoid setting the price or terms first as it will only increase on the counter offer. Always try and find out what the other party is offering and come in with a counter offer yourself. The same can be said of negotiating a salary for example for a new job. Always keep the trump card up your sleeve.

Exercise Tip#8

Think of a negotiation you may have had and take note of what your expected and ideal outcome was and what you ended up settling for. Then ask yourself the following questions.

    a) Was the outcome what you expected?
    b) Is there anything you could have done to get a better deal?
    c) Who were you negotiating opposite?

In the light of the above answers identify one personal skill or trait that you can improve to become a better negotiator. Once you identify this, carry out some online research as to how you can address this issue and commit some time to work on this.

Life tip #9
THE SOLITUDE OF LEADERSHIP

Many books have been written about leadership and all aspects of leadership. Yet there is one aspect that is seldom looked at or looked at from a different perspective. More often than not, any reference to leadership will outline the loneliness attached to any leadership job. Be it the top job of a Prime Minister or the CEO of a company or the head of a family unit. When there is a leader you will always find that leader will have moments of what is often referred to as loneliness. I have often been in such situations myself yet rather than looking at it from a loneliness perspective I would rather look at it as solitude. The two are often linked but do not mean the same thing.

Loneliness indicates isolation and anxiety and is not a state people enjoy. Solitude on the other hand is an important aspect of our lives that we often disregard despite being crucial to our decisions day to day. In an ever connected world it is easy to feel lonely and difficult to find solitude. Yet, there has never been a more important time for our leaders to seek solitude so as to be able to stop and think and take good decisions.

Leaders are crucially dependant on the people they lead. Yet it is these same people that will be their downfall if they choose to. This is why it is crucial for a leader to be able to move away from the group without distancing himself/herself so as to maintain a healthy perspective as well as give him/her the time to reflect and lead the group effectively.

SCENARIO #1 Think of a Prime Minister leading a cabinet of Ministers. In a Westminster style system the Prime Minister is 'Primus Inter pares' which is he/she is a first amongst equals. The decisions are always taken at a collegial cabinet level, which shares responsibility, yet most of the very tough decisions as to appointments and final word are down to one person. Naturally, this calls for difficult situations which require any individual occupying this position to be collegial on the one hand, yet distance him/herself on other issues that require tough stands. It is these decisions that require a retreat into solitude. The same scenario can be applied to any CEO or leader of an organisation. Often one refers to these positions as the loneliest jobs in the world. In this respect, it is not so much loneliness, rather, the solitude of the job that is crucially important. When big decisions have to be taken in positions of leadership they are often solitary decisions.

SCENARIO #2 Think of parents of a large family or even a small family. In this day and age the delineation between parents and growing teenage children is becoming blurrier. Gone are the days when 'children should be seen and not heard' was the parenting norm. The increasing grey area due to parents and children acting more like friends oftentimes creates moments of tension due to the parent suddenly recognising that he/she should be the disciplinarian or the leader of the family. It is at moments like these that one realises on a micro level how important the idea of solitude and distance is. Let us take this example onto a macro level, as a leader running his/her business. Closeness to the employees is crucial to be able to rally a team around you and push through your decisions, yet familiarity can oftentimes breed contempt, and one has to be careful not to blur the lines too much between engaging with employees and leading them.

WORKING ON TIP#9

Solitude is a state that leaders require and opt for out of choice because of the group dynamics that they operate within. A leader thrives on solitude because it gives her/him the space to think and decide responsibly. Human nature leads us wanting a leader but can drag a leader down. If the leader is too close to the group his/her leadership will inevitably struggle. There is a fine line between the group and a leader which is a balance that is always required. The moment this is understood, then leadership can flourish as well as the group one is trying to lead.

> **Exercise Tip#9**
>
> Find some time to distance yourself from your group be it at work or at home or in your community. Look at the dynamics that you are working within and try and recognise situations within which you are required to take the lead. Take a deep breath and seek some solitude for yourself and far from the madding crowd. Take note of what you have been doing and what you have managed to achieve and if need be redress the way you operate within the group. Harness the power that solitude gives you and use it to your advantage.

Life tip #10
IT'S NOT WHAT WE SAY BUT HOW WE SAY IT

In a world of high connectivity we are tending to communicate less in person and use the written word more and more be it through e-mail or electronic messaging or simply by using emojis. Often this sort of communication is so instantaneous that it is done without thinking. Have you ever received an email and depending on what mood you were in read it quickly and reacted only to go back to it later in the day and realise there may have been a different twist on it depending on what tone you used when reading it? This is the same thing that happens in our daily lives. We communicate through our words yet often forget that our tone of voice and body language are just as important.

SCENARIO #1 Take for example a receptionist. He/she greets thousands of people on the job and is the first impression of a company. Any good receptionist knows that the job requires them to ensure a friendly disposition at all times, irrespective of the caller or visitor. Their every move is scrutinised to ensure the company is well represented. This is the first port of call for many. The first impression. Funnily enough we all hate it when we walk into a doctor's office and are greeted by a grumpy, off putting receptionist. That first impression dictates how we are going to feel about the appointment and the doctor's clinic. Reality is that you don't get a second chance for a first impression. Turning the tables onto ourselves however, is not that obvious to many. How do we behave and what impression to we give off when we say good morning or engage in a conversation with someone?

SCENARIO #2 You are out at dinner and from the onset the waiter was offish and rather abrupt. When he/she leaves the menus and walks away you comment about his/her attitude and lack of customer service. After a couple of minutes he/she is approaching your table to take your order. This has set the scene for a dinner experience which could go either way and because of the waiter's tone of voice and uncomfortable first impression you are automatically put on edge. You now have a choice; go with the flow and repay the wrong attitude with more of the same or rise above it and go beyond. You go for the latter and irrespective of the waiter's attitude you are polite, courteous, engage and order with a smile. Suddenly the waiter reacts positively to this and goes with the flow. You end up having a great dinner and the service was great. A simple change that changed everything and determined the outcome of your evening.

WORKING ON TIP #10

Depending on the situation, your mood on the day or your personality you are constantly in a situation where you could change the course of a discussion, a greeting or a difficult conversation simply by changing your tone of voice or choice of words or through your body language. Oftentimes we spend time choosing our words for a given situation without bothering with the tone we should attribute or how we should position ourselves. To many this is obvious and is often passed off as natural charisma. How do you explain how some people can send people to hell and back and actually have them enjoy the ride? It's not as hard as you think. Recognising this can actually make a huge difference to the outcomes of your conversations.

LIFE TIP #10

Exercise Tip #10

For this tip the most important thing is to be aware of who you are meeting and what you are saying but most importantly how you are saying it. Try doing things slowly. Instead of walking into work or the beauty salon or the bank with your phone in your hand, try walking in hands free. Walk in straight and remove your sunglasses and look people in the eyes and say 'good morning' or a similar greeting before you engage with anyone. You will see the change automatically and recognise their disposition to be open to you from the outset. It's a question of the vibe you give off when you first meet someone or before you engage with an individual that will make all the difference.

Life tip #11
80% OF YOUR FEARS WILL NEVER HAPPEN

Some people live life on the edge, throwing caution to the wind and living day by day expecting the unexpected and dealing with it as it comes along. Others adopt a more cautious approach and others simply live their lives worrying about every minute detail. In reality, a simple exercise will teach you that a good 80% of all we care to worry about never happens, which begs the question as to why we worry at all.

SCENARIO #1 You wake up in the morning with a pounding headache. Last night you went to bed worrying as to whether your alarm would ring and wake you up for a really important meeting. As you get up you worry whether you will make the appointment on time or whether you will get stuck in traffic – the same traffic you pass through every day. The next on your list is whether the suit you have picked out is smart enough. Will my tie match or my tights tear on my way? Your thoughts paralyse you and slow you down. With each glance at your watch you realise you have planned ahead knowing you had this meeting, knowing there will be traffic. Ultimately, the anxiety you have caused yourself is for absolutely nothing. Your headache will affect your performance at your meeting and possibly the outcome. Was that worthwhile?

SCENARIO #2 I know of many parents who tell you that as soon as you know you are going to become a parent your worry starts and never ends. Will my child be born healthy? Will they speak? Will they walk? Later in their years, will they struggle to learn? Will they have friends? The list goes on and on. Even in their late teens and twenties we worry as to who they hang out with, who they will marry if at all, which job they will choose, will they be happy? We worry so much oftentimes we lose sight of what we should be doing in the first place – being a parent. Teaching our children from day one, the skills they will need to be able to make the right decisions which will not worry us so much. Yet, how many of us actually stop to think in this way?

WORKING ON TIP#11

In reality 80% of your worries and negative thoughts will never materialise, yet by verbalising and thinking about them you create a fear factor that inadvertently traps you into a negative cycle which inevitably attracts more negative outcomes in your life. Actually, you are not more unlucky than your next door neighbour or your best friend – it is the way you deal with difficult situation and your reaction to them that often makes them look bigger than they actually are. There is nothing intrinsically wrong with being cautious or careful, or looking at the worst case scenario and planning for it. What is counterproductive is keeping your fears and thoughts within you as though they are about to happen any time – living in fear of what is to come thus not being able to live life to the full. Thinking about problems in advance has no tangible solution which begs the question as to why we worry about issues that may not even happen in the first place.

LIFE TIP #11

> ### *Exercise Tip#11*
>
> Take a three day window and keep a little notebook and jot down every worry that crosses your mind during this time frame. Wait a few days and look back at the list and see how many of your little worries have actually materialised in a longer time-frame. Take note to refer back to this list six months or even a year later. You will realise that a small fraction of your list actually materialised and you dealt with them as a matter of course with no lasting consequences.

Life tip #12
DON'T JUST THINK IT, INK IT

It is incredible that when you actually write things down, scribble your thoughts and plans you create a better and clearer line of thought. I am not relating this to just business and work plans but even for personal thoughts and positions that can benefit from being put down by a pen to paper.

The process of jotting things down may surprise you. There is something more to the act of writing; your thoughts trigger off your muscles to transfer these thoughts in drawings, letters and words. Often, the bigger the paper the better the process of thought. Techniques often used in brainstorming sessions or for group work can easily be used for our personal lives. It is true that our phones and tablets have in many ways tried to replicate our need to brainstorm and list things down. The applications available are quite genius. They prioritise, keep you posted, remind you yet they still don't have the

LIFE TIP #12

commitment level that a handwritten list has. It's as though by writing it in ink you are committing yourself to actually working through the list. It is also useful to carry around a handwritten list and tick off what you have achieved and scribble down some more.

SCENARIO #1 Have you ever cleared up or started packing up your old room and came across an old diary of yours or old scribbles with thoughts on them. Incredibly, you have kept them all these years and refuse to throw them away. Incredibly, they reveal a part of your soul that you have long forgotten yet recognize. Inevitably, you stop what you are doing and just sit there reading through the pages. Your first crush, a heartbreak, a fight with a friend, your first day at work. Each page is full of your most intimate thoughts and feelings contemplating how you are dealing with the challenges life throws at you every day. Looking back at these thoughts you will realize that just by writing them down you were committing yourself to working through those daily battles. The actual process of putting pen to paper helped you work through some difficult teenage years. Even today, you will find that by writing a letter, even if you do not intend to send it, to someone who has hurt you, is therapeutic in itself and allows for a better command of the situation you are facing.

LIFE TIP #12

SCENARIO #2 Towards the end of the year in December many of us tend to come up with one or two New Year's resolutions. Fast forward two or three months into the year and most of what we resolved is long forgotten. Alas, we don't even remember what our resolutions were. Enter, the written list of things to do that year – it's tangible with measurable and specific goals. You actually sit down with a pen and paper and write down a list of nine things you wish to do during the year. Each one can be ticked off as you go along and the list can be used for referencing, reducing, adding as well as prioritizing things you wish to do. The pressure of a written list and the commitment it actually signals is much greater than having it listed on your phone or computer and simply forgotten about. You go back to it a couple of times throughout the year and you update as you go along. The next year you review it and bring forward any items that you did not manage to do if you are still interested in pursuing such.

WORKING ON TIP #12

Think of your childhood and reconnect with the wonderful fantasy of Christmas lists. Your letter to Santa, which asked him for all things wonderful, many of which you would find under the tree on Christmas morning is nothing more

LIFE TIP #12

than a wish list. Think of this wonderful tradition today. It is still a written letter and a written list. It's still magical and most parents will admit to keeping these letters or at best taking a photo of them for posterity. The act of actually writing down your lists connects your psyche through your arm and finally the pen and paper. It's like you are transferring energy to the paper that commits you to what you write. Can you imagine a letter to Santa on a computer or an email? The magic is gone. There is something magical about lists. Discover it. It is something that can transform the way you look at life.

Exercise Tip#12

Switch off your mobile devices and your television and get yourself a little pocket diary or simply a piece of paper. Stop to think and list four things you wish to get done in three months. Don't exaggerate, start slowly. The things to do cannot be generic and must be specific and measurable. There is no in between or grey areas. Within three months you can only mark as done or not done. Once compiled, leave the list and look at it in a few days. Add and erase as you please and slowly start prioritizing. Which one will you do first and how are you going to do it? Slowly weave this process into your daily routine. Much like checking your Facebook, you will also check your list. Three months down the line, cross check it and see what has been done. Those items on the list that you haven't achieved may not have been achievable or should not be there in the first place.

Life tip #13
THE BIG FISH SMALL POND SYNDROME

This syndrome is symptomatic of small communities, be they small states or small communities. In brief, it refers to the phenomenon of power and importance with the wrong attitude within small communities which runs the risk of blinding those that actually achieve it. In reality, a position of power, when mismanaged within a small community is nothing more than a big fish in a small pond. Transfer that big fish into a larger pond or the ocean and the fish becomes a small fish.

SCENARIO #1 Think of a local journalist for a local newspaper. His stories make the front pages every week. The entire community knows of him and greets her as some sort of celebrity. The Mayor of the town quotes his work and he is his top choice for the tough interviews. In a few years he has made it to the top of his career. His next move is out of

LIFE TIP #13

her local community and into the big city. He signs up for a larger regional newspaper and immediately realizes that he is now one of many good journalists and can consider himself to be very lucky if his work features at all in the paper. What is worse is that nobody recognizes him in the street. Nobody even knows that he is a journalist.

SCENARIO #2 A neurosurgeon comes back to her hometown. She made a name for herself overseas and has amassed a considerable size of wealth. Her hometown needs her and she has decided to come back home. The size of the place has always amazed her yet she could do with a calmer pace of life surrounded by genuine and good people with few hidden agendas. The community soon begins to idolize her. Her husband is the centre of all things social and the family becomes an important icon in the little community. Soon, the doctor and her husband become the untouchables. Their arrogance grows as they increasingly fall into the trappings of a small community. Caught up in it has a blinding effect on their attitudes and from loving people they start pushing people away. It's all about their attitude and how they have related to being a big fish in a small pond. They could have done the opposite, stay humble and recognize their effect on a community yet realizing that this was only the case because of a small community.

WORKING ON TIP#13

In reality, the situations described above are more common than we would like to admit. Had we to apply them to different scenarios in our lives such as our family environment or work environment, we will soon realize that the minute we distinguish ourselves from a group, become more popular, better or more successful, there is a serious risk of us falling into the big fish small pond cycle.

Exercise Tip#13

Think of a situation which you are in where you feel you are admired more than those around you, or you are in a better position. Should you not find one of these situations, think of a friend or colleague or an old acquaintance that has fallen into this trap. Then ask yourself, whether this situation is one that you have embraced and recognized as a responsibility or one that has pumped wind into your sails and allowed you to act stronger and more powerful, in some cases unkind and rather nasty.

Write a few points down as to how you feel you should be acting as opposed to how you are acting and work on a plan as to how you can redress the situation.

Life tip #14
SEE FOR THE FIRST TIME

Have you ever looked at old photos of your childhood home or a place you haven't visited in a while? The tiny details simply pop out of the page. The intricate details of the railings, the buildings and door knobs simply jump out at you. The experience is incredible. It's similar to touching down in a new country. Driving around a new place, with an open window you are bound to breathe in each and every detail. Have you ever tried to do this in your day to day life? Have you ever tried to put on a fresh pair of eyes to your day to day environment? To your home? To your office and yes why not to your partner and children?

SCENARIO #1 Every day we commute to work and back. Every day we wake up and sleep in the same house and each and every day we go through pretty much the same routine and motions. The other day, my neighbour asked me to take care of her two kids for a couple of hours. They are 6 and 9 years old and like most children they are energetic and inquisitive. They came home and I could see them scan everything until the questions started rolling in. They pointed at personal items and wanted to know what, where and how. They spent a lot of time looking at the photos we have hanging on the wall and they wanted to know who's who. With that came streams of stories of my earlier days and the stories of personal items, many of which I had forgotten. These details fascinated them and when they left I realised that life has become so fast that we are missing out and not noticing details any longer.

SCENARIO #2 Last summer I took some foreign friends out on my boat for the day. I planned to give them a good overview of the coast and some of my favourite spots. I frequent these places often yet being out at sea, one switches off, as one does, and I was looking forward to it. As we motored out of the marina, something struck me almost immediately. My friends where visibly excited, eyes wide open, absorbing and looking at every detail of the coast, island and sea around us. I started pointing out the various sites and details to give my friends a great tour. In doing so I also started noticing details and coastal features that I never saw, even though I had passed that coastline numerous times. I had literally forgotten how to look with awareness and depth and not only look for the sake of looking.

WORKING ON TIP#14

As we have seen we can easily get used to our surroundings to the point that we miss out on the beauty of them as well as ignore the flaws. It's like living life on auto-pilot. The most important aspect of this Tip is actually recognizing that this happens. Once you have realized that you are going through the motions each and every morning you will automatically slow down and become more aware of your surroundings as well as the people around you.

Exercise Tip#14

Take stock of your day to day routine and dedicate some time to keeping your eyes and ears open. Commute to work and look out of the window in all directions. Observe and listen. You may notice a new shop that has opened or one that has closed. Listen to the sounds and smell the aromas coming from the street vendors. With each passing day you will realize that your commute to work is not as monotonous as it once was. The same could be done with your colleagues or friends. Sit down and listen to them. Ask questions. Take a step back and see what you receive. Do be aware however, that you may realize in time that what you liked about your colleague or friend may now have the opposite effect on you. The same could be said in reverse. How are your friends and colleagues perceiving you?

Life tip #15
WHY GRIT MATTERS?

Grit is not a word many of us use on a daily basis. Most of us are able to identify a person with 'grit' yet struggle to put our finger on its true meaning and relevance. To me, grit is courage and resolve with a bit of an adverturer spirit thrown in. It is an individual's strength of character and value base, which identifies them from others. Those possessing grit have more stamina, determination and motivation to achieve long-term goals and overcome the adversity that they will inevitably face. It's that something extra that people possess to go the distance. Grit is a quality that you are able to develop. It is innate in all humans. It's much like our survival instinct and it's not ambition.

SCENARIO #1 Think of a middle-aged man or woman. Life is catching up with them when they decide to join a running club. The beginning is a slog. Each morning they get out of bed for their early morning run. Each morning the aches and pains get stronger. The first month is tough yet the finish line is getting closer. The marathon is the ultimate challenge. The long-term goal to actually run the marathon brings out an individual's grit. It's this grit that lifts them out of bed each morning. It's this grit that gets them there in the end.

SCENARIO #2 You are in your early twenties and decide to set up your own business. To begin with the banks refuse to loan you the money to set up. They tell you something about you being too young and inexperienced and a risk. Many would give up at this stage, yet you believe in your idea and you keep pushing. You look for investors and each week dress up in a suit and give a presentation to potential investors. Most shut the door and ask you to leave not even giving you the chance to sell your idea. Each day you tell yourself the same thing. 'It only takes one investor' and keep on trying until one day you find someone willing to invest. This is grit – the determination and belief in yourself to get there no matter how hard it is. It is the same grit seen in world class athletes, in children learning how to walk or ride a bike. This is the grit I am speaking about.

WORKING ON TIP#15

One can develop grit by being flexible and open to tackling issues. Grit is most useful during challenging times and

LIFE TIP #15

times of adversity. It is at times like this that you recognize how important this determination and staying power is to the outcomes in your life. In reality, one can prepare for these trying situation by ensuring that you do not live your life constantly in your comfort zone. Taking a leap of faith and moving out of your comfort zone allows you to stretch your limits and face your fears in a way that you wouldn't, thus developing your innate grit which will serve you so well when you truly need it. In hindsight, you will then see that what was a challenging move and jump into unchartered territory eventually becomes your comfort zone. You think back and you smile to yourself. Then it's time to push again...

LIFE TIP #15

> ### *Exercise Tip#15*
>
> Evaluate your current position within one of your ongoing environments, be it at work, your personal development, in sports, or within an organisation you are part of. Get a notepad, take a snapshot of where you are, identify and note your comfort zone and draw a circle around this. Now draw an outer circle similar to a doughnut and list things which are outside of your comfort zone. Select one or a couple of these things and then come up with a plan as how you can tackle these, attributing a time line to it.
>
> Conquer your fears and take a leap of faith. It will stand you in good stead sooner rather than later.

Life tip #16
YOU CAN BE YOUR WORST ENEMY

Most of us go through life surrounded by people and oftentimes dependent on those same people. Increasingly in a highly digitized and connected society, we depend on what people think of us without stopping to realize that what is most important is what we think of ourselves. – The Power of YOU. You are your best friend but can also be your worst enemy. You, and you alone have the power to empower yourself or to drag yourself down. The sooner you are aware of this, the quicker you are able to take control of your life and actually start determining where and how you are going to get there.

SCENARIO #1 You are in a job which has gone stale. You realize that it is time to leave but you are so comfortable you cannot ever imagine yourself moving. You love your colleagues, yet you realize that if you are going to grow you need to move

LIFE TIP #16

on. Your colleagues keep reminding you how comfortable you are and how easy familiarity is. A part of you is pushing you to start searching for a new opportunity, whilst the other half is pulling you back. You can seek all the advice in the world. You can listen to all those little voices in your ear yet ultimately it is you who will decide whether to take the plunge or otherwise. You are the only one to decide whether you wish to be your best friend or worst enemy.

SCENARIO #2 You have decided to travel a little and leave your community for a while. You are still not sure you're escaping the hold your parents have over you or a broken heart but either way it's good to get out. Change perspective and 'find yourself'. Many of your friends have settled down and are planning their weddings. Without realizing it, they try hard to convince you to stay and not leave. If you hear the word 'escapism' another time you will surely scream. A discussion with yourself leaves you with one clear direction – to get out and travel for a year or so. Break with your routine and see where life takes you. You finally listen to yourself and as you do you feel empowered as though you could conquer the world. Once away, life is not easy. There are ups and downs, yet you start trusting your instinct more, and relying more on yourself. You make yourself your best friend and for this you grow into a stronger and better version of you.

WORKING ON TIP#16

In life we will make many friends and a few enemies. Throughout different periods of our life we will seek different groups of friends. The older you get the more you realise that you have less and less real friends. How many friends are we in touch with from our childhood? Can we even relate to them today? Ultimately, the only constant friend in your life is YOU. It is up to you to decide whether you will be your best friend or worst enemy. Be as good to yourself as you wish people to be good to you.

LIFE TIP #16

Exercise Tip#16

Find some alone time, possibly after spoiling yourself a little with a massage, a facial or a spa. It could also be some time for you to finish that book that has been collecting dust on your bedside table.

Write a list of the following:
1. What can I do each and every day that gives me joy alone?
2. How do I relax?
3. What are my strengths and weaknesses and how can I help myself be better?
4. What are my opportunities and which ones are worth pursuing?

Then write down a shorter list with a maximum of five points outlining your best qualities and what makes you YOU. Pat yourself on the back and enjoy the person you are. Celebrate yourself and think of how you can become a better you.

Life tip #17
FOOD FOR THOUGHT

Our relationship with food will always be a complex one. Some of us have a love affair with food, others a pretty average one and others have a strained and difficult relationship. Our relationship with food can often be traced to our childhood but is also reflected in how we view ourselves. Growing up in a home where food is important with a parent that can cook will naturally provide a platform for their children who will appreciate food more than those that have been brought up on a culture of eating just for the sake of eating. In reality, food is one of the simple pleasures of life. It brings out our character and zest for life. The experimentation with different flavours and aromas allows us to break the mould and expand our palette, much like thinking out of the box and living life on the edge outside of our comfort zone every so often..

SCENARIO #1 Think back to one of the earliest memories of your childhood. It is most certainly related to food. Be it that ice cream you had all summer long, or a typical dish, your grandmother used to make each Sunday. Each smell conjures memories of a childhood by the sea, or high up in the mountains. Each memory is precious as it brings back a sense of belonging and understanding of your past. Just like the time your father taught you how to make his favourite pasta sauce and added just enough chilli to tingle your tongue. Or when your mother helped you bake cookies or a cake for school. There is no doubt that food will always be an important aspect of our lives, one that we should embrace and cultivate.

SCENRARIO #2 Food can also bring back some very strained memories for us or reflect some very uncomfortable times. You will also notice that the times when you had a strained relationship with food were your toughest patches. The time you decided to go on a crash diet, or the other time you over ate only to realise you had put on a few kilos and didn't know why or how. Realising and accepting that your relationship with food is directly related to how you are feeling about yourself is one crucial and important aspect of ensuring you live a balanced and content life.

WORKING ON TIP#17

Depending on which culture you come from you are bound to have a different relationship with food. I will never forget my time helping my dad cook over the weekend. These times instilled a love for food and the skill to cook a good meal. Nonetheless, our appetite for food can also evolve over the years. Growing older and lifestyle habits go hand in hand with food and at times what you eat becomes who you are. Personally, I have over the years, become a more conscious eater and I now do not eat meat, eggs or dairy. I feel better but what works for me and doesn't necessarily work for the other. Yet, we should all be more aware of what we eat, how our body responds to the food we eat and how food is crucial for a substantial existence.

LIFE TIP #17

Exercise Tip#17

Choose a particular week of the month and take note of everything you eat. Keep a food diary and jot down each item. With each annotation take note of the mood you are in when you eat and your stress levels from 1-5. At the end of the week take a look back and identify where you could have restrained yourself or what more food you could have had. Understand your habits and work to ensure a better balance and hence a better relationship with food. Learn to understand how food affects your body. Understand what is best for you by being more in tune with yourself.

Life tip #18
TECHNOLOGY AND PATIENCE

Advances in technology over the last decade have brought about a radical change to our lifestyles. Changes in the way and speed we communicate has not only changed the way we interact but has also altered our expectations and concepts of time. This has resulted in an expectation of instant gratification which in itself is not a bad thing unless this expectation is not accompanied by a rationalisation that not all aspects of life can be instant. Unfortunately, this is not generally the case. The 'everything now at the touch of a button' syndrome runs deep into our psyche today and we often expect the same to happen with all aspects of our lives.

SCENARIO #1 Think of your first love. Think back at when you first saw him/her and how you felt. Think of what you would have done had you not had a mobile or tablet handy. You would have gone out of your way to get to know him/her. Found a quiet moment to speak to them and have a drink. Each week you would find a way of meeting or exchange notes through a good friend and possibly sneak a call or two when your parents were not hogging the fixed line. Your courtship was slow and steady. You took it in stages and really thought about where you were going to meet and what you would say. Transport this into the technological age. Before speaking face to face you have already checked out his/her Facebook page and through photos or comments have already made out what makes him/her tick. You've probably already touched base on messenger and started exchanging face time calls. The once a week meeting becomes an everyday affair. This is definitely convenient yet also feels as though you are on fifth gear all the time. The issue with everything being so fast is that a true and meaningful relationship can actually escape you. You may look great on your social media pages but what is underneath cannot be reflected in a photo or a post. This is where patience is most important. Human relationships take time and investment. They are complex and difficult at the best of times and cannot be run over by technology.

SCENARIO #2 Have you ever upgraded your phone and lost a large chunk of your contact numbers? This is the most terrifying thought for many of us. You frantically check your whatsapp messages to try and figure out whose number is whose. A multitude of calls come in with number unknown and you have no idea who is calling you. Frustrating is an understatement. You post a note on Facebook asking friends to send you their mobile numbers so that you can start collecting them once again. For a second you wish you had the old fashioned mini-address book in your bag. How on earth are you going to cope? You need to call your mother but you don't even know her telephone number by heart. Why would you? SIRI used to do all the dialling. Rewind a decade ago and you still remember all your friends' landlines. Our minds were wired to remember numbers. Today, many of us don't even bother. Our patience and will to retain this sort of information has simply disappeared.

WORKING ON TIP#18

In a faster paced world, it is crucial for us to take stock of our patience scale. How patient are we? Can we sustain long queues or complain that it should all be done on line. Have we got the patience to go round a supermarket to buy our groceries or is online shopping easier and quicker? Are we patient enough to genuinly wait a couple of hours for someone to reply to our text or email?Our patience threshold is different depending on what we have been used to.

LIFE TIP #18

Exercise Tip#18

Email has revolutionised the pace and turnaround of communication at work. Most expect an email to be replied to within that same day or within 8 hours. If you don't get a reply you start bouncing at your computer. On the otherhand, we receive emails and most of us are not patient enough to open such emails when you finish working on whatever you are working on. Hence, we are constantly distracted and letting the flow of emails dictate our focus.

1. Deactivate the 'email received' sound on your computer and phone;
2. Deactivate the email summary and notification from your inbox on your computer;
3. Be patient and disciplined to access your emails at pre-determined times or when you finish a particular task.

If you don't work with emails you can apply this to text or what's app messages.

There is no excuse. If its really urgent people will eventually call!

Life tip #19
SHARE YOUR PLANS AS MUCH AS YOU CAN

Plans are a staple of any individual's life. We plan our studies, our careers, our families and our businesses to name but a few. Many times we will only discuss our plans with our nearest and dearest for fear of failure or for a mixture of reasons, be they lack of confidence or a fear that they may be copied. In reality, there is a great benefit of sharing our plans and thoughts with as wide a variety of people as possible. To begin with, you never know where your best idea will come from. People will comment, analyse, shoot your ideas down yet with each new suggestion or criticism your idea can grow and develop. You open yourself up to the benefit of other people's experiences. Secondly, sharing your ideas and plans gives you an insurance of not backing down. It's like a bit of public pressure for a commitment that you will follow through.

SCENARIO #1 Have you ever sung in the shower at the top of your lungs? No doubt you have. Most sing in the shower. Some of us are tone deaf yet for some reason we are all incredible singers when under flowing water. If truth be told, a few are indeed incredible singers under and out of the shower yet lack the basic confidence to actually expose their voice to the world. Show it off and allow for some criticism and development. The same can be said for our ideas. Whilst we are happy being our own critics and possibly our harshest critics, most of us are not geared up for the impending criticism, some justified, some not, that comes with bringing our ideas to the fore. What we do not realise is that by exposing your plans to many people you are also refining them and committing to them. Keeping them under wraps may lose you a great opportunity.

SCENARIO #2 You know that ideally you should stop smoking. You are finally at the edge of smoking your last cigarette. A part of you wants to confide with your partner, friend or colleague that you intend to call it quits. Yet, with each cigarette you question and doubt yourself that you will be able to follow it through and really quit. You have been there before and by relapsing you feel that you are failing and losing face. Hence, you stay quiet, and either quit but relapse after a few days or you don't try quitting at all. Reality is that you are quitting smoking for yourself and no one else yet its another factor unrelated to smoking that is now also introduced into this equation. On the otherhand, when you are ready share your idea and decision to stop smoking with as many people as you can. Turn a concern and this pressure to your advantage and use it to help you get through the first 21 days. The more you discuss it the more you develop it and in time, the more you commit to it.

WORKING ON TIP#19

Any discussion with people will require you to develop your network of people and gain confidence in actually discussing with people, irrespective of how random this can be. Life is a network of intricate relationships, some deeper than the other, some we nurture, some are there are we know that they will always be there. Used well, social media is actually a great place to maintain your networks. For some reason just by browsing through your newsfeeds you feel connected to those who are on your Facebook page even though you haven't seen them for a while. You are in touch with their lives and know more about them than you would have if you were not linked. Harness this link to be able to connect and share your ideas.

Exercise Tip#19

Write down one or two plans that have been brewing in your mind for a while. It could be a plan to lose weight or to set up a small business. Discuss these plans with a few people outside of your close family network and see how it develops. Then, after discussion jot down the ideas that have come out of your discussion and build on your plans. See where it takes you.

Life tip #20 — SOME BUSINESS TIPS

At one stage or another work could be an integral part of one's life and in a way even when in employment there is still a business and entrepreneurial side to how you operate. The following are my top 10 business tips which I learnt by experience, and mostly the hard way.

TIP #1 Not everyone gets it. If you have an idea which you are willing to share and discuss with others you must be prepared for the inevitable. Not everyone will get it. They will be sceptical, punch holes in it and be dismissive, yet this does not mean it is not a good idea.
IN BRIEF – If they don't get it, don't be discouraged. Use their ideas to make your idea better and communicate it in a different way.

TIP #2 Identify what drives you. Think and write down in short, succinct phrases, all that motivates you. This will be the basis and outcome of most of your decisions.
IN BRIEF – find out what makes you tick. This is what will drive your actions and decisions, both the good and the bad ones.

***TIP #3* Always be prepared with an exit plan.** Be creative and develop your ideas in business and at home, yet always keep in mind that they can go wrong and managing that is much easier if you are prepared with an exit plan. I am not suggesting being negative but rather being positively cautious.

IN BRIEF – Plan for success but also for failure or better, for a less damaging escape.

***TIP #4* Keep it real, keep it simple.** Whenever you embark on a project or idea, keep your feet firmly on the ground and recognise that you will not see incredible success overnight. Hard work, a reality check and simple plan will get you through the toughest times of starting something new. This basic approach will allow you re-evaluate and rethink when you need to as well as push forward or hold on the breaks when is needed

IN BRIEF – keep it real, keep it simple.

More on the power of simplicity

Have you ever sat through a lecture and walked out thinking – well they could have said it in five minutes more effectively. Oftentimes, we overcomplicate our speak, just like we would overcomplicate our food thus ruining the overall experience. For some reason we have been brought up thinking that using complex words makes us sound more highbrow, when actually they only serve to confuse our message more. Less is more in conversations. Stick to the simple facts and get to the point as people's attention spans are actually quite short nowadays.

TIP #5 Strategize your meetings. Meetings are part and parcel of any business person's daily routine. The opportunity to discuss face to face is unique and you should always go prepared and manage your meetings so as to assist with the outcome you have in mind. Yet, before accepting any meeting, where possible ask for more info as to why the meeting is being called and what is required from you. In this manner unnecessary meetings will be instantly addressed or you all go one step ahead and better prepared.
IN BRIEF – Create and conduct proactive meetings.

More on meetings

Technology has advanced at a rapid pace, with online meetings a common occurrence in today's boardrooms. Despite all, however, most prefer face-to-face meetings. Many do tend to drag on without actually reaching a conclusion, so over the years I have religiously asked for an agenda prior to any meeting ensuring that we do not talk around an issue but get to the point and work toward a solution.

TIP #6 Don't become a workaholic. Think of any person on their deathbed. The last thing they will say is that they regret that they didn't work harder or stay at the office longer. Usually, their regrets have to do with the simpler more gratifying things in life. Work hard if you have to but always create a good mix with the things you enjoy doing. If you have forgotten what these things are, take some time out to discover them and work around them. Find something that you are passionate about, something other than work. If you are in a relationship then ensure your partner is part of your down time. This is not about creating a life-work balance. This is about being able to prioritise accordingly.

IN BRIEF – don't become a workaholic and be able to prioritise.

TIP #7 Accounting matters. I have never really liked accounts yet having timely accounts is crucial. It is useless cringing each time you come across a set of accounts or leave it in the hands of others. It is crucial that you gain an understanding of the numbers behind your business and are able to question them.

IN BRIEF – Get your accounts in order and make them add value.

***TIP #8* Build your team as opposed to building a team.**
The key word here is 'your' as it has to be a team composed of people that fit your style, strengths and weaknesses. You are as good as your team. You are as good as the weakest link in your team. The best teams are those that complement each other. Don't surround yourself by people who have the same skill set as you. Success takes a variety of skills, the sum of which you should build your team around.

IN BRIEF – Identify your needs and choose your team accordingly.

More on teams

People with experience are an important factor to a team, yet don't underestimate those without. They have to start from somewhere. Both are important on a team. The first will bring experience, yet also bad habits, the second is a clean slate with no experience yet energy and fresh ideas you may not have thought of before. Sometimes you should gamble and see if it pays off.

***TIP #9* Choose your partners** – When starting out, you are rearing to go and may be willing to compromise on the basics as long as the partnership gets off the ground. Don't be fooled. It is crucial at this stage, to choose your partners carefully and ensure that what drives them is the same thing that drives you as in the medium to long term these differences is what will drive you apart.

IN BRIEF – Choose your partners wisely.

***TIP #10* Go for it.** Ultimately, there is no secret formula to a successful business. You need to put your head down and get on with the job. Worst case scenario you always have your exit plan and are minimising your exposure.

IN BRIEF – Just do it.

Life tip #21
LEARN TO LET GO

Life and our decisions always look much easier in hindsight. We often wish we could have the benefit of hindsight when taking decisions, especially tough decisions. Some we nail, others we will regret and carry with us throughout our lives. In reality, this is the process of learning. As a one year old learning to walk will get up when they fall, so do we get up and move on from a bad decision. Can you imagine what will happen to a one year old if he/she refuses to try and walk just because they fell? This is what happens to you when you refuse to let go and forgive yourself for a mistake that you have made.

SCENARIO #1 You have just gone through a painful separation and simply can't get over it. It is not the ending of your relationship that you find tough to handle but the niggling feeling of failure and anger at yourself for being where you are at the moment. Without going into the merits if it was doomed to fail, if it was your partners or your fault, reality is that the marriage broke down. At this stage you have a choice. Will you live your life never forgiving yourself and never letting go?

LIFE TIP #21

Allowing your decisions to determine the rest of your life? Or will you let it go, learn from your decisions and use it as a lesson to make sure you don't make the same mistakes?

SITUATION #2 Think of something you have built up, like a business or a home for you and your family. The day finally arrives, when you have decided to sell out of your business or sell your home. To begin with, the decision could be enticing for the financial gain but is still a tough one. Psychologically it is very tough, as this is what you have built over the years. There is a lot of attachment to it and selling was never going to be easy. Despite all, you know this is the best thing to do at the time and you sell out, only to realise a few months down the line that you may have rushed or undersold and had circumstances been different you would have done it a different way. This makes you cling onto a decision you took which you may not wish to let go of. It conditions the way you take decisions now as you fear making a second mistake.

Working on Tip#21

Taking a decision is never easy, especially when they are big, life changing decisions. We are often blessed with a little more life experience when we do take these big decisions, which doesn't make it easier, only more comforting that we may be taking them for the better. It is experience and conviction that allows us to take good decisions. Any decision, however will have its downsides. What is crucial is that you are fully aware of each consequence before you take a decision. Much like an exit plan for a business idea, for you to be able to sit comfortably with your decisions you need an exit plan for your decisions.

Exercise Tip#21

Before taking a decision take some time out and have a paper and pen handy. Make a list of the pros and cons of taking a decision. Leave it for a few days, or hours if you do not have that luxury, and go back to your list. On the basis of this list take a decision and ensure that you take it and don't turn back. Keep the list if you fear regretting your decision so that you can go back to your list and understand the circumstances within which you actually made that decisions. Hindsight plays funny tricks with our minds and may cloud our judgement when it comes to taking decisions. In this way you can adopt a no regrets policy as to why you have taken a decision, which is the best policy to use when letting go.

On the otherhand, if the decision has been taken and you feel that you can't let go then you need to coach yourself through this process and work at it. See for yourself what helps you move on and reinforce what works and avoid situations or thought that that get you thinking again.

Life tip #22
SABBATICAL AT FORTY

We tend to associate sabbaticals with teenagers or twenty year olds taking a gap year before starting or just after finishing university. What we do not realise is that such breaks in our lives and routines are more important when we are older and are in need of a good physical and mental break. The idea of a long break is often alien to a 40-50 year old. It is seen as an impossibility rather than a necessity.

SCENARIO #1 You are in a career that has dominated your life for almost twenty years. It has had its ups and downs yet given you great satisfaction and reward. The stability and routine is something that you cherish. Vacation Leave is an alien concept to you unless really necessary. A day of leave means a day of unanswered emails and even if you wish to take a day off you make sure you have email access at all times. Without realising it you have become dependent on that lifeline of emails. Your phone ringing and messaging work is what reminds you that you are valued and are valuable at work.. You decide to take a short break on the insistence of your partner. Three days maximum is your absolute limit.

LIFE TIP #22

Three days away from the job ... yet you take your laptop with you 'just in case' something happens. It rarely does, but just in case. Does this sound familiar? It probably does as most of us fall into this rut early on and never quite get out of it. The holiday is a success yet you get back even more exhausted than you were before. The break in routine didn't quite did quite the opposite to your nerves. It would do, seeing that a few days are simply not enough to recharge your batteries. The first day back in office you are already back to your old self and its like you never went away.

SCENARIO #2 You wake up one morning and realise that you can hardly get out of bed. A visit to your doctor indicates that you are suffering from exhaustion. Still not understanding how this came about you are forced to take a mental and physical break. Initially, you feel helpless and trapped. You experience increasing withdrawal symptoms of your hectic lifestyle which only make you more tired rather than easing your condition. This persists for a few weeks until the third or fourth week when you start feeling much better and more alert. It is at this time that your rest actually begins. Unfortunately many of us are only ever driven to taking such a long break and possibly longer when we are forced rather than by choice, not realising the importance and benefit to our health, lives and yes our work when we actually do take time to take stock and breathe.

WORKING ON TIP#22

Reaching our forties is a time to wake up to the reality that we are no longer twenty. We no longer have the energy and tenacity of a teenager and our priorities are radically different. It is a time to look back but also to look forward. More quality time is one area that we look to and crave for. We discuss it and wish it but rarely take active steps to make it happen. There is always one excuse or another which prevents us from taking a long break. Money is usually the largest excuse, children, family, work commitments. Irrespective of the excuse they remain excuses. When you look at some of the wealthiest members of society you will realise that money is not really the excuse they find as they don't have this excuse.

LIFE TIP #22

> ### *Exercise Tip#22*
>
> Take a look at the last twenty years of your working life and take note of any long breaks that you have taken apart from your honeymoon or breaks in between jobs. Take note of how long the break was and what you did during this time. Now take a look at the year ahead and look at the possibility of taking a lengthy 4 week break - a complete break, away from your emails and work and routine. Ideally you should plan longer term to extend this break to a sabbatical of at least six months. This is a good time to reinvent yourselves, plan ahead, work on new ideas, get back in shape and yes why not, relax.

Life tip #23
THE ART OF FIRING PEOPLE

Firing someone from your place of work or from your life is never easy and more often than not will leave a trail of bitterness and resentment. It doesn't have to be this way though. Relationship building and honest brokerage when dealing with people are ways in which you can actually get to the stage of firing someone and have them thank you for your honesty. The decisions taken before firing someone and throughout the actual process and after can alter the way you fire an individual and also make a huge difference to that person's life.

SCENARIO #1 You have just been informed that you are required to fire a member of staff for poor performance. It is probably one of the worst parts of the job but one that has to be done. Over the years you have managed to perfect the art of firing using the same philosophy which is that of ensuring that those you fire leave your room in full recognition as to why they have been fired and being able to make a fresh start. In this case, the member of staff is arrogant and defensive when you come to fire him/her. They do not give you the time to speak and hardly allow you any explanation time. You wait patiently for the right time, and simply say 'the reason I have not been able to explain why you are being fired is exactly the reason you are being fired. I would love to sit down and explain this in more detail after you have calmed down as this would make a difference to the way you approach your next employment.' And with that you allow space to think.

SCENARIO #2 You are sitting across a young member of staff who has not settled in their job. The conversation is a difficult one as you know you could get it very wrong. Before you could say anything the member of staff asks you whether you are kicking them out and you acknowledge the fact. Their reaction is not a good one but you proceed to explain the reasons behind the dismissal armed with the facts in hand. Slowly but surely you establish trust between you and the member of staff and proceed to advise them how they can work out their failings and learn from this experience. The experience is a good one to the extent that you are thanked for your honesty at the end of the meeting.

WORKING ON TIP#23

In line with other Tips within this notebook, reaching the stage where you can get to dismiss a member of staff gracefully is not something that is innate. Oftentimes it is easier to distance ourselves emotionally from the event due to its high emotional content and difficulty. It is however counterproductive to think that being cold and emotionless throughout a dismissal is the best way to go. With each difficult conversation, you are extending your brand as a caring and empathising individual. This process is one that takes time and requires particular attention to the person you are facing. Fostering a culture of learning and development as well as performance is also a requirement for good and effective conversations. Whereas this tip focussed on dismissing someone at work, not all of us would be in such a position. Nonetheless, most of us will encounter similar situations in life outside the realms of work.

Exercise Tip#23

Take a look at a difficult conversation you have had over the last year. It could be with a friend, family member or with a member of staff. Think about what you would have done differently in hindsight and how you could have transformed the conversation into an opportunity rather than a difficult conversation.

Life tip #24
REWARD YOURSELF AT MILESTONES

We all feel good when we are rewarded with a compliment or a random gift. It's enough to make our day brighter, change our mood or even motivate us to do something good ourselves. Most times we wait for others to shower us with praise or acknowledge our success without stopping to congratulate ourselves once in a while.

SCENARIO #1 I was once involved in a tough legal issue which had become messy and dragged on for years. It was physically and mentally exhausting yet I felt I had achieved a milestone. As with most court cases they tend to take their toll on you. I decided soon after the case ended that I should do something to celebrate and tap myself on the back. Technically I did not win the case but we settled out of court and I ended up paying out but I felt liberated and happy and refused to allow the case to get to me. I had suffered years of aggravation and stress and felt I deserved something special. Having decided to give myself some attention I proceeded to go out and buy myself a watch I had wanted for a while. It may sound consumerist yet the feel good factor was real and made me realise that every so often we should indulge and spoil ourselves upon our milestones.

SCENARIO #2 You decided later on in your years after having children to go back to studying and found a course that really interested you. You were under no illusions as to how easy or difficult it was going to be. The course was an evening course and had to fit into your daily routine. Slowly but surely you gained the confidence to sit and study, sit for exams and get through the course. Graduation came along and your satisfaction was through the roof. Time for a break now and a tap on the back, you quickly book yourself a holiday with your partner. A weekend break to celebrate your success.

WORKING ON TIP#24

Celebrating our success is not as easy as we think. We are great at supporting others but we are often our most vocal critics and keep at it irrespective of our success. It is often our lack of appreciation for our small and big successes that holds us back. We have often read and watched documentaries about maintaining a positive mental attitude throughout life. It is time to actually look at fostering a culture of giving ourselves a positive break every now and again. A tap on the back, a gift or a pep talk in the mirror. The inner strength it gives us knowing that we are supporting ourselves and are proud of ourselves can go a long way.

Exercise Tip#24

Take some time and work on a short list of things you are proud of having done over the last year. Analyse them and see whether you stopped to congratulate yourself enough and recognise your success. Identify who you shared this success with and how you processed it. Take stock, then look at yourself today and what you are working on. Identify which of your projects, small or big, are going to give you a boost when concluded and work toward finishing them off. Promise yourself a break or a gift once they are done and see how this motivates you.

Life tip #25
PEOPLE WHO KNOW DON'T TALK. THOSE WHO DON'T KNOW TALK A LOT

I believe that there are two types of people in this world. Those that think they know it all and those that know that they don't. Often, the latter are those that will seek knowledge and experience from others, testing their convictions and theories and working through them rather than trying to impose their ideas and understanding on others. These are also those people who tend to speak less and be less vocal and listen more. This doesn't mean that talking is wrong. On the contrary, it is important to discuss and debate as well as to impart your experience and understanding of things, yet always maintaining a balanced view point and listening to what others have to say rather than cutting them off before they have said it.

LIFE TIP #25

SCENARIO #1 You find yourself in a board meeting surrounded by people from different areas of business. You are feeling slightly intimidated, yet know that this is your one chance to get them to understand your business plan and possibly take a chance on you. You look around the room and analyse the characters that you have to work around. There are those that are very vocal, speak all the time and hardly allow anyone to get a word in edgeways, there are those that don't say a word, and a few that listen and analyse before speaking. Almost immediately you can tell which individuals you have to convince first and after listening to everyone you draw upon the few ideas that have emerged that you can work with, always keeping eye contact with those important few you have to convince.

SCENARIO #2 You are with a group of friends arguing a point. Tempers flair as one of the most vocal keeps on hammering his/her point home without realising that there may be another perspective. Without wishing to insult or hurt anyone, you soon realise that the conversation is really going nowhere and if not tamed will easily deteriorate into a flinging match of personal insults. Generally, when one loses an argument it can easily become personal. Realising this you quickly move in to calm the waters after having listened carefully, managing to eliminate the personal attacks and working on the areas of agreement. Slowly but surely, the conversation calms down and has taken no hostages.

WORKING ON TIP#25

We have all fallen into the trap of thinking we know best and we have the best solution to a given issue. In reality, experience will teach us that irrespective of how much we know there is always something we do not know and unless we are able to open up our minds to such possibilities then we risk becoming a victim of our own mind. *We have two ears and one mouth so that we can listen twice as much as we speak. – Epictetus.*

Exercise Tip#25

Next time you are around a board room table or around your kitchen table with friends, make it a point to sit and listen. Don't speak, don't argue your point, just sit and listen to the others making the arguments. Understand what they are saying and look at it from their perspective. Even if you disagree with them, try hard to understand where they are coming from and see if you can bridge the gap between what they are saying with what you think and what the others are saying. You will soon notice that not only have you learnt something from the conversation but are able to play a more constructive role during meetings or discussions.

Life tip #26
IT IS NICE TO BE IMPORTANT BUT IT IS IMPORTANT TO BE NICE

We go through life trying hard to make a success out of it albeit our definition of success is not necessarily the same as those around us. Some of us are important people in society, some less so, however we all represent something to a group of people and are important to a group or more than a group. Oftentimes we concentrate more on this point rather than understanding that whilst there is nothing wrong in being important, there is a lot that is wrong with not being nice. The two can and should go hand in hand.

SCENARIO #1 It is your first day of work and you are as expected nervous and a little bit on edge. You walk in and meet up with the Head of Human Resources who is friendly and

LIFE TIP #26

takes an interest in you, empathizing with the fact that it is actually your first day. You have a meeting scheduled with the Managing Director and the Management team which you are particularly nervous about and with reason. You walk in and nobody acknowledges you. It's business as usual. In your mind you are wondering when anybody in the room would acknowledge you. It never happens. As far as the room is concerned there is an agenda and it is business as usual. It could not have hurt to say hello or introduce you, yet this is the way things are done. You wonder 'are the people around the table this important to the point that they cannot even be nice?'

SCENARIO #2 You have a board meeting you are not particularly looking forward to. There are a few big and important names around the table and you are nervous as to the presentation you are about to give. You are there early enough to set up and wait until the members start arriving. Each one greets you with a smile and introduces themselves indicating how happy they are to finally meet you and looking forward to hearing what you have to say. This makes all the difference. Your nerves decrease and you feel positive to lead the way. Simple gestures are all you need to change the way you feel.

WORKING ON TIP#26

Think of the way you act around people. Take a look at your behavior and the attitudes of those around you and understand how you can be a nicer version of yourself. Start with the simple things like saying hello and taking an interest in the people you meet. Common courtesies go a long way. Almost immediately you will see that people react to you differently. Irrespective of how important and how busy you are you should always work on the small details that will have you stand out.

Exercise Tip#26

The next time you are in a group of friends or in a meeting, take note of the way people interact with you and with others. Make it a point to ensure that you go out of your way to be friendly and nice. Even if you are putting across a difficult point there is a nice way to do that so work on the way you come across and how people perceive you. Also check in with a few friends and ask for feedback as to how you come across and take their feedback on the chin.

Life tip #27
YOU DON'T CHOOSE YOUR FAMILY

If you stop to think for a few minutes you will realize that the old quote stating that 'you don't choose your family' rings quite true. You are born into a family with little choice and are pretty much stuck with your parents and siblings throughout your life. Growing up together makes you a little part of each other yet also individuals. For the better part of your life you try hard to differentiate yourself from your family members, yet the family element is still very much present. Your expectations from your family members are generally higher than those from your friends and acquaintances, causing friction along the way. The way I look at it is whilst it could be great to have family around it is a bonus if you actually get on with them as you would friends you choose. This is a fact that once accepted will make you happier around members of your family and less expecting of their behavior.

LIFE TIP #27

SCENARIO #1 It's Christmas Day and you are trying to work out how the day will pan out with young children. Christmas is a time for celebration with family and is fast turning into a seriously stressful day of the year. Not only are you concerned with your children and their celebration but you also have to deal with your parents and their plans for you and your siblings who you do not necessarily get on with. It's nice to spend a day of the year together but have you ever thought why you only get to spend one or two days a year with your entire family. If you got on better you would not need Christmas to come around to see them. Your day is exhausting - a visit to your maternal grandmother, then the other side, only to have to visit your partner's family after lunch. The end of the day cannot come sooner.

SCENARIO #2 Growing up you always clashed with your older brother. He bullied you or always thought he was better than you. You couldn't wait for him to leave you alone and tried your utmost to get away. Finally, he left the house to get married. The house was all yours. Your parents were all yours. There were a few things you missed about him, like his clothes or music yet you were now the master of your own castle. He didn't come round too often stating he was far too busy and this suited you fine. Your relationship never really took off yet he was family and as far as you are concerned you will always be there for him. Slowly but surely, you rekindled your relationship. He would never be your best friend. He would never be the one you would confide in, yet you have come to terms with this fact and take it as it is. When you meet you can have a laugh for old times' sake without having to expect anything more. As a result your relationship is better than it would ever have been.

WORKING ON TIP #27

Accept your family members for who they are and who they wish to be. Stop having unrealistic expectations from them and go with the flow. Your life will be much more peaceful and your relationship will actually grow. When you are around the table, just accept the fact that your sister will not get up to wash the dishes and if you feel you want to then do it without passing a snide remark. If your brother was never generous he is not about to show up with a large plant when you invite him over and neither should you expect it. Each one of us have our quirks and differences and the earlier we relieve the pressure of being a family member and just accept our family for who they are the better our relationships will be with our parents and siblings.

Exercise Tip#27

Take a look at your family members and make a note of the things that irritate you most about them. Leave the list for a few days and add to it as you go along. On the flipside, make a note of the things that probably irritate them about you. After a week sit down and have a long and hard think. Are they issues that really affect you life? How do you react to them and how difficult would it be for you to simply accept them? Then make a list of what you expect from your family. A list of behaviors that you feel they should have toward you and that you feel you are lacking. Again, analyse whether you would expect the same from friends and work backwards. Are you expecting too much? Is the pressure you are putting on your relationships with family members unrealistic? How can you change that?

Life tip #28 — MEET THE MONKEY

There are hundreds of great reads out there. 'The One Minute Manager meets the Monkey' is a handbook by Kenneth Blanchard that has had a great influence on my management style with respect to daily tasks, people and delegating. In a nutshell, think of all the issues people come to you with and have a look at how you handle those issues. Often, you would take on the problems of other people and handle them yourself, hence taking the monkey off their back and putting it on yours. In the end, you find yourself with many other people's monkeys with no time to actually deal with your own.

SCENARIO #1 You are leading a team and have always thought of yourself as an active leader with great problem solving skills. People come to you naturally because you are so reliable when solving other people's issues. Each day you take on the solution of a few problems. Initially you do it with great ease realizing that it takes you a fraction of the time it takes others to actually solve their problems. Slowly but surely you become the

LIFE TIP #28

go to person and before you know it you have overloaded yourself with other people's issues which are taking up precious time from the solution of your own. This is when you realize that whilst you can meet other people's monkey you should never take ownership of it.

SCENARIO #2 Have you ever stopped to think about your relationship with your friends or family members. You are always at the other end of the line for those needing a helping hand or stuck with a problem. Your friends are going through a separation your house is their first port of call. Your parents need something you are the one they call. Irrespective of how busy you are you are constantly carrying other people's monkey's on your back until you realize that you actually have taken on too much. Until that day when you are not invited to a dinner party by the same friends who actually passed on their monkey to you a few times. It is at this stage that you realize that there actually is another way.

WORKING ON TIP#28

My suggestion to you is to read the book and learn how to tackle the monkeys. Visualize it, communicate it to your team and your circle of friends and use it so as to contribute to their enrichment and development. What you will realize is that they do not need somebody to actually do it for them but someone to guide or ensure that they first try to do it.

> **Exercise Tip#28**
>
> Buy the book and read it. Then make a list of the monkeys you have on your back and identify which ones are yours and which are not. Then ask yourself. Those monkeys that are not mine, how many could I have actually have not taken?

Life tip #29
ABOUT MINDFULNESS

We often make the mistake of confusing religion with spirituality. The two can of course co-exist but they can also exist independently of each other. One can embrace religion as well as choose to live without it and become more spiritual. Others prefer the concept of a higher sense of self-awareness and or mindfulness. There is no right or wrong, what is important is the understanding you achieve of who you are and why you are here and use this to move forward and do the best we could.

SCENARIO #1 Life was never meant to be easy. Over the years we learn how to cope with the different tools that are given to us, how to overcome difficult situations and how to deal with others to which there are no solutions. Probably one of the hardest things to deal with is the death of a loved one. Overnight, a piece of your heart breaks down. The pain is physical and the feeling of despair deep. Many who believe in a religion will turn to prayer to ask, to question to find the answers they require. Others like myself, will turn to my spiritual side which I have learnt to tap into. I work on rationalizing my grief and looking beyond it and make it work for me. There is no easy solution, and there is not one way of doing it. We are all different and respecting the different ways of working through our lives is a first step.

SCENARIO #2 You are invited to a yoga session which will include a session on mindfulness. This is something you were never really attracted to but decide to go with a friend. As you enter the class you feel transported to another era. You do not feel like you fit it yet you are willing to give it a try. Armed with a mat and a good mental attitude you resist the urge to leave and try it for the first few minutes. It is all a little bit alien to you. Without realizing it you actually start working on your awareness and consciousness. Admittedly, it is quite scary to begin with, yet you feel a certain amount of peace. After the first session you decide to keep going back and even find yourself working on some of the exercises at home. You find you create a little space of heaven for your mind and thoughts and funnily life seems that much easier to work through day by day. You slowly discover your spiritual self. Slowly but surely it gives you comfort.

WORKING ON TIP #29

Be open to new ideas and new ways of thinking and working through your daily lives. Find your own style and what works for you. This doesn't necessarily mean ditching what you have been brought up with, the norms and standards by which you have lived your life over the last forty years. It may lead to this eventually if you wish it to, but it doesn't have to. Be adventurous and take on new ideas and tasks. Allocate some time to learn more about breathing exercises and meditation. There are a lot of great and free resources to get you started. You never know where it will lead you. It will be fun. It's a way to discover yourself. To discover your spiritual side. To find that with yourself you are never quite alone.

Exercise Tip#29

Take a look at your life and see what you do that gives you comfort. What do you do in times of crisis? Who do you look for? Do you pray? Do you reason things out? Do you pick up a book and try and find answers or solicit the help of a dead relative? Have you ever tried meditation? Are you aware of your breathing? Whichever path you choose to take, find a way of exploring it to the maximum. Find a way of owning it and making it work for you. Discover the spiritual side to your being beyond the accepted norm. Try and make mindfulness your natural mental state, and as defined; 'achieved by focusing one's awareness on the present moment, while calmly acknowledging and accepting one's feelings, thoughts, and bodily sensations, used as a therapeutic technique'.

Life tip #30 — MORE THAN WORDS

Not all words are created equal. We also tend to have a small pool of words that we repeatedly use. Yet some words are more powerful than others. Being aware of such words and using them in the right manner is key. These words will act as a catalyst and help maintain the right mindset.

SCENARIO #1 You are going through one of your biggest and toughest periods of your life. One might argue that it's all relative and indeed it is. Whatever the project, issue or problem you face this is creating a large amount of pressure, stress, uncertainty, anxiety and worry. Yet, you know that in the long run this will pass and you will be able to overcome all this. It could also be that you have brought this pressure on yourself and the outcome is and could be a positive thing. Yet, it's tough and the mind and negative thoughts are taking over your daily routine. There are days when you manage to overcome this stress but there are other days when you are completely knocked out.

WORKING ON TIP #30

Think of past challenges, issues, problems or projects that you have had to handle in the past? Probably you have to think hard to list a number of these. Some will be easier to recall and others slightly harder. Now think of how you felt at that time whilst going through these challenges. Did you at the time think that this was the biggest problem or challenge you had to overcome? Did you stress out? Did you think or feel that there was no solution? Now fast forward to how you eventually sorted or overcome these challenges. Recall how time also helps us move on. Come back to the present challenges and reposition and reframe these.

Exercise on Tip #30

Think of the challenge, issue, problem, project that you are currently facing. Get pen and paper and draw up a list of words reflecting particular skills and traits that you need to overcome this challenge. Write as many words as you can. When ready read them out loud. These are more than just words; this is a description of your required mindset. From this day on, you will touch base and relate to these words when you feel low or insecure.

ACKNOWLEDGEMENTS

To Christian Peregin and Jo Caruana.
Thank you for your time and energy.
Thank you for making it fun and challenging.

To Mikela Fenech Pace
Thank you for editing the way you did.
Thank you for being a catalyst in making it happen.

To my family, in-laws and friends.
Thank you for being there.

To my wife Lara and stepdaughter Sara.
Thank you for being an integral part of my journey.
Thank you both for being you.

And to You.
Whoever and wherever you are,
Thank you for reading #Forty.

Jonathan Shaw
@bookForty
Fortybethechange
#Fortybethechange